EVAN PLACEY

Evan Placey is a Canadian-British playwright who grew up in Toronto and now lives in London, England. His plays include *Girls Like That* (commissioned by Birmingham Repertory Theatre, Theatre Royal Plymouth and West Yorkshire Playhouse); *Mother of Him* (Courtyard Theatre; winner of the King's Cross Award for New Writing, RBC National Playwriting Competition, Canada, and the Samuel French Canadian Play Contest); *Banana Boys* (Hampstead Theatre); *Suicide(s) in Vegas* (Canadian tour; Centaur Theatre Award nomination); *Scarberia* (Forward Theatre Project/York Theatre Royal); *How Was It For You?* (Unicorn Theatre); *Holloway Jones* (Synergy Theatre Project/schools tour/Unicorn Theatre; winner of the Brian Way Award 2012 for Best Play for Young People; Writers' Guild Award nomination) and *Pronoun* (National Theatre Connections). Work for radio includes *Mother of Him* (BBC Radio 3/Little Brother Productions). Evan is a Creative Fellow and Lecturer at the University of Southampton, and also teaches playwriting to young people for various theatres, and also in prisons.

Other Titles in this Series

Mike Bartlett
BULL

Tom Basden
HOLES
JOSEPH K
THERE IS A WAR

Jez Butterworth
JERUSALEM
JEZ BUTTERWORTH PLAYS: ONE
MOJO
THE NIGHT HERON
PARLOUR SONG
THE RIVER
THE WINTERLING

Caryl Churchill
BLUE HEART
CHURCHILL PLAYS: THREE
CHURCHILL PLAYS: FOUR
CHURCHILL: SHORTS
CLOUD NINE
DING DONG THE WICKED
A DREAM PLAY
after Strindberg
DRUNK ENOUGH TO SAY
I LOVE YOU?
FAR AWAY
HOTEL
ICECREAM
LIGHT SHINING IN
BUCKINGHAMSHIRE
LOVE AND INFORMATION
MAD FOREST
A NUMBER
SEVEN JEWISH CHILDREN
THE SKRIKER
THIS IS A CHAIR
THYESTES *after* Seneca
TRAPS

Stella Feehily
BANG BANG BANG
DREAMS OF VIOLENCE
DUCK
O GO MY MAN
THIS MAY HURT A BIT

debbie tucker green
BORN BAD
DIRTY BUTTERFLY
NUT
RANDOM
STONING MARY
TRADE & GENERATIONS
TRUTH AND RECONCILIATION

Declan Greene
MOTH

Nancy Harris
LOVE IN A GLASS JAR
NO ROMANCE
OUR NEW GIRL

Lucy Kirkwood
BEAUTY AND THE BEAST
with Katie Mitchell
BLOODY WIMMIN
CHIMERICA
HEDDA *after* Ibsen
IT FELT EMPTY WHEN THE
HEART WENT AT FIRST BUT
IT IS ALRIGHT NOW
NSFW
TINDERBOX

Conor McPherson
DUBLIN CAROL
McPHERSON PLAYS: ONE
McPHERSON PLAYS: TWO
McPHERSON PLAYS: THREE
THE NIGHT ALIVE
PORT AUTHORITY
THE SEAFARER
SHINING CITY
THE VEIL
THE WEIR

Chloë Moss
CHRISTMAS IS MILES AWAY
HOW LOVE IS SPELT
FATAL LIGHT
THE GATEKEEPER
THE WAY HOME
THIS WIDE NIGHT

Bruce Norris
CLYBOURNE PARK
THE LOW ROAD
THE PAIN AND THE ITCH
PURPLE HEART

Evan Placey
GIRLS LIKE THAT

Jack Thorne
2ND MAY 1997
BUNNY
LET THE RIGHT ONE IN
after John Ajvide Lindqvist
MYDIDAE
STACY & FANNY AND FAGGOT
WHEN YOU CURE ME

Enda Walsh
BEDBOUND & MISTERMAN
DELIRIUM
DISCO PIGS & SUCKING DUBLIN
ENDA WALSH PLAYS: ONE
MISTERMAN
THE NEW ELECTRIC BALLROOM
ONCE
PENELOPE
THE SMALL THINGS
THE WALWORTH FARCE

Tom Wells
JUMPERS FOR GOALPOSTS
THE KITCHEN SINK
ME, AS A PENGUIN

Evan Placey

PRONOUN

NICK HERN BOOKS
London
www.nickhernbooks.co.uk

A Nick Hern Book

Pronoun first published in Great Britain as a paperback original in 2014 by Nick Hern Books Limited, The Glasshouse, 49a Goldhawk Road, London W12 8QP

Cover image: John McAreavy for West Yorkshire Playhouse
Cover design: Ned Hoste, 2H

Typeset by Nick Hern Books, London

Printed and bound in Great Britain by Mimeo Ltd, Huntingdon, Cambridgeshire PE29 6XX

A CIP catalogue record for this book is available from the British Library

ISBN 978 1 84842 391 6

For Danny

Author's Note

While the play was written for a cast of seven, with the same actors who play the main characters also playing the additional characters, larger casts could certainly have separate actors play these roles (or could increase the number of the Senior Management Team). So the play could have anywhere from seven up to any number of actors. In either case, there should be a heightened awareness with the latter characters that these are young actors playing adults – that this is performance: when they first appear, we watch an actor put on an apron to become Mum, an actor put on a doctor's coat, etc. But once they're 'dressed', they needn't worry about playing the gender or age of their character, merely the truth of that moment.

Dean is a transgender male – meaning Dean was born a girl, and is biologically female, but identifies as male, and in transition to becoming male. In the stage directions, Dean is referred to as *he* as this is the pronoun that Dean, if he were real and not in a play, would go by and identify with. The role should be played by a female actor.

Set – it's imagined that somewhere on stage (or maybe the whole stage) is a closet/wardrobe/clothing rack… or maybe a dress-up chest. Somewhere from which the actors get items of clothing on stage to become the adult characters.

Also, on stage is a large poster of James Dean from *Rebel Without a Cause*.

The play takes place from May 2013 to June 2014.

Acknowledgements

Anthony Banks, Rob Watt, Lucy Deere, Paula Hamilton, Tom Lyons, and all the staff at the National Theatre. James Grieve and Michael Fentiman.

Tanya Tillett at the Knight Hall Agency.

The staff and young people at Gendered Intelligence. Also the brilliant resources on their website, particularly 'A Guide for Parents and Family Members of Trans People Living in the UK' and 'A Guide for Young Trans People in the UK'.

Jamie, for the insight, openness and anecdotes.

Rebel Without a Cause by Steward Stern, Irving Shulman and Nicholas Ray, from whom I have quoted lines. And the screenplay for *Breakfast at Tiffany's* by George Axelrod, based on the book by Truman Capote, for the same reason.

The many young people who took part in the premiere productions of this play. You give me hope for the future.

E.P.

Pronoun was commissioned as part of the 2014 National Theatre Connections Festival and premiered by youth theatres across the UK, including a performance at the National Theatre in July 2014.

Each year the National Theatre asks ten writers to create new plays to be performed by young theatre companies all over the country. From Scotland to Cornwall and Northern Ireland to Norfolk, Connections celebrates great new writing for the stage – and the energy, commitment and talent of young theatremakers.

www.nationaltheatre.org.uk/connections

Characters

THE TEENS

DEAN, *transgender male (female-to-male); played by a female actor*

JOSH, *male*

KYLE, *male*

AMY, *female*

LAURA, *female*

DANI, *female*

JAMES DEAN, *male. As in the movie star… circa 1955,* Rebel Without a Cause *teenager look: blue jeans, white T-shirt, red jacket. Speaks with an American accent.*

ADDITIONAL CHARACTERS (THE 'ADULTS')

MUM, *forties, played by a young male*

DAD, *forties, played by a young female*

SMT (*Senior Management Team*), *played by two to four actors*

DOCTORS (MONROE, BOGART, BRANDO), *played by three actors*

PRIVATE DOCTOR

A Note on Punctuation

A forward slash (/) denotes a line that is interrupted, and the point of interruption.

A dash (–) is a cut-off, sometimes of one's own thought with a different thought (not a pause or beat).

An ellipsis (…) is a loss or search for words.

A lack of punctuation at the end of a line means the next line comes right in.

Words in square brackets are not spoken, but there to clarify a line's meaning.

Scene One

AMY*'s bedroom.* JOSH *wears a dress. He looks in a full-length mirror.*

KYLE. What the fuck?

JOSH. For nothing in the world.

KYLE. What?

lots of short words, very modern, and casual, relatable for a younger audience

JOSH. For nothing in the world, will I swear not to arm myself.

KYLE. What?

JOSH. Will I swear not to arm myself and put on a man's dress.

KYLE. Josh.

JOSH. Who said that?

KYLE. What?

JOSH. Who said that?

KYLE. Said what? Josh, why are you –

JOSH. For nothing in the world, will I swear not to arm myself and put on a man's dress. Who said it?

KYLE. Rihanna?

JOSH. Joan of Arc.

KYLE.... Okay.

JOSH. But in history, sir overlooked that bit, why she was actually condemned to death, y'know.

KYLE. Josh?

JOSH. Yeah?

KYLE. You're wearing a dress.

JOSH. Yeah.

KYLE. Okay.

JOSH. Yeah.

KYLE. So you're aware, you're aware, that you're wearing – I thought maybe.

JOSH. No. I'm aware.

KYLE. Right.

JOSH. Amy rang when you were downstairs. They're out of pineapple so she's replaced it with mushrooms, which in my mind isn't really a comparable replacement, one's a fruit and the other's – and she's got it without cheese, which actually entirely defeats the purpose of ordering a pizza if you ask me.

KYLE. Dude, why the fuck are you wearing a dress?

JOSH. I dunno. I thought. Thought it would help. Understand, y'know.

KYLE. And?

JOSH. Nothing.

KYLE. At least you look pretty.

JOSH. You think?

KYLE. Shows off your legs.

JOSH. Thought somehow, if I, like there'd be this moment, it would just click, that I'd feel how she, how he… but I just feel like a boy in a dress.

KYLE. You used to wear eyeliner and mascara.

JOSH. For like a week.

KYLE. Three as I recall.

JOSH. That's not the same.

KYLE. Your emo days.

JOSH. It's not the – this isn't how it was supposed to go. This wasn't part of the plan.

KYLE. Every plan has variables, mate.

JOSH. You go away for a shitty two-week holiday for Easter with your annoying family to some three-star shithole in Benidorm, you expect to come home with a sunburn, you expect to come home with diarrhoea, you expect to come home with a pen that has a picture of a woman on it whose clothes fall off every time you click it – what you do not expect when you come home is to find your sixteen-year-old best friend engaged and that your girlfriend is…

KYLE. Come here.

JOSH. No. What are you –

KYLE. It'll help. (*Puts eyeliner on* JOSH.)

JOSH. We were supposed to – there were so many things we were supposed to do, that we'd planned to do. After next year, gonna spend our gap year together. Travel Thailand.

KYLE. You still can. (*Gets lipstick, starts to put it on* JOSH.)

JOSH. How are we –

KYLE. Stop talking.

Push your lips together.

JOSH *looks in mirror.*

Anything?

JOSH. No.

KYLE *gets on one knee. Holds out a ring box.*

The fuck you doing?

KYLE. Joshua Robbins.

JOSH. Kyle.

KYLE. We've known each other a long time now.

JOSH. Kyle, get up.

KYLE. Ever since I first spotted you having pissed your pants by the sandpit in nursery, I knew. I knew then you were the one. Joshua Michael Robins, make me the happiest groom and be my best man? (*Opens box, it's a Haribo sweet.*)

JOSH *takes it, eats it.*

Is that a yes?

JOSH. I love you, man.

KYLE *picks* JOSH *up, spins him around, whooping.*

KYLE. It's gonna be ace. Here. (*Envelope.*)

JOSH. What's this?

KYLE. Your duties as best man. I've put a tick-list in.

JOSH.... Terrific.

JOSH *gets distracted by himself in the mirror again.*

KYLE. It'll be alright, man.

JOSH. It'll be great.

KYLE. I meant about.

JOSH. Oh.

KYLE. Josh?

JOSH. Yeah.

KYLE. Amy'll be back any minute, and [if] she finds you in her room she'll castrate you with her bare teeth. Trust me, I've got the teethmarks. It still hurts when I pee. (*Exits.*)

The song 'Everyday' by Buddy Holly begins to play.

JOSH *takes off the dress. On the other side of the mirror (somewhere else),* DEAN *enters in boxers and a sports bra/vest top. Faces himself in the mirror. The effect being that by this point* JOSH *too is in his underwear – the two of them looking at each other through the mirror.*

Beat.

JOSH *exits.*

Scene Two

Continuous from Scene One.

DEAN*'s bedroom. A large poster of* JAMES DEAN *from* Rebel Without a Cause *on the wall.*

DEAN *retrieves a needle. Fills it with liquid from a small tube. Squirts the end of the needle gently. And reaches round and confidently injects himself in his bum cheek.*

He then wraps a large roll of bandage around his chest, binding his breasts so they're flat. Puts a T-shirt on. Looks in mirror.

Puts another T-shirt over top of the first.

Gets a sock. Puts it in his underwear, adjusts it.

Puts on some skinny jeans and Converse.

Hair product in his short hair.

Douses himself in Lynx. The ritual is complete.

JAMES DEAN *appears. The music stops.*

JAMES DEAN. Hey, kid.

DEAN. I look crap.

JAMES DEAN. Take it easy.

DEAN. Do I look crap?

JAMES DEAN. You look swell.

DEAN. Fuck off swell.

JAMES DEAN. You look a bit like me, kid.

DEAN *looks at the poster of* JAMES DEAN, *then at the* JAMES DEAN *standing there.*

DEAN. You're totally photoshopped.

JAMES DEAN. There was no such thing then. It's all me. C'mon. It's time for your jab, buddy.

Draping arm around him, the two looking in the mirror.

DEAN *throws off his arm, feeling insecure when looking at them both side by side.*

DEAN. I already took it. Buddy.

JAMES DEAN. Whoa. I'm not the enemy, Dean.

DEAN. No, you're just some dumb dead guy I talk to.

JAMES DEAN. No need to get personal 'bout it.

Shouting is heard.

What's that?

DEAN, *unhappy with his appearance, changes the T-shirt for a button-down shirt instead.*

DEAN. *That* is why no one should get married. *That* is why some people shouldn't be allowed to have children. *That* is the alien life forms also known as Mum and Dad.

JAMES DEAN. 'She, she says one thing, he says another, and everybody changes back again,' right?

DEAN. Some things haven't changed.

DEAN *looking at himself in profile again.*

JAMES DEAN. Too big.

DEAN. What do you know?

JAMES DEAN. Well I've got one for a start.

DEAN. You're not even here.

JAMES DEAN. You're the one talking to me.

DEAN. It's the T. It's messing with my head.

Beat.

Takes the sock out from his trousers.

JAMES DEAN. Told you.

DEAN (*throws it to him*). Put a sock in it will you.

JAMES DEAN. Touché.

DEAN *puts a smaller sock in.* JAMES DEAN *lights a cigarette.*

DEAN. Don't you know smoking can kill you?

JAMES DEAN *laughs*. [*I'm already dead*.]

Touché.

JAMES DEAN *joins him at the mirror. Both of them side by side checking themselves out in profile. Fixing their shirts*.

DANI *enters*. *She stands there for a moment watching before* DEAN *notices her.*

Beat. JAMES DEAN *watches the rest of the scene unseen by* DANI.

DANI. They're shouting as per usual.

'Once upon a time'

This is clearly a game they used to play/story they used to tell as kids.

DEAN. 'there were two kids who learned they were in fact royalty'

DANI. 'who were in fact abducted by the people they thought were Mum and Dad'

DEAN. 'so they left their screaming parents and went to live in the castle'

BOTH. 'and lived happily ever after.'

Beat. DANI *still lingers in the doorway.*

DEAN. You can come in.

DANI. Can I?

DEAN. You've always been –

DANI. It's different now.

DEAN. … No.

DANI. Yes.

DEAN. … Yes.

DANI. Looks good. The shirt.

DEAN. You think?

DANI. Matches your eyes.

DEAN. / Thanks

DANI. / Almost wouldn't know.

Almost.

Doesn't it bother you?

DEAN. . . . No.

DANI. No. You don't even know what I'm asking. *No*. Some things don't change. *No*. You were always scared of me. Meant to be the other way around. You're the older one. And even now.

DEAN. What do you want, Dani?

DANI. Doesn't it bother you? How everyone's chatting shit about you?

DEAN. No.

DANI. No?

DEAN. I couldn't give a damn.

DANI. *Couldn't give a damn*. You're so goddamn American sometimes.

DEAN. I don't care.

DANI. Well I do. I give a damn. You remember at primary. When people were chatting shit about you. Saying about you and what's his name, Brad, douchebag, saying how you'd, and I stood up for you. Even though you were the older one. When they were saying 'Hear your big sister's a right' – I stood up for you, fought for you. No one said nothing to me 'bout you after that, once I told 'em what's what, showed 'em what's what.

DEAN. Okay.

DANI. But now I can't say nothing. Cos this time the shit they're talking's true.

DEAN. I'm sorry that you're… I'd never want you to… because of me.

DANI. … I know.

Pause.

Let's have a look at you then.

Are you happy?

DEAN. Yeah. I am. I'm. Getting there.

DANI. Okay. (*Goes to leave. Changes her mind. Turns back.*)

Dean?

DEAN. Yeah?

DANI. You can pretend all you want, but you'll never have a dick.

Scene Three

MUM *and* DAD *appear. We watch as a male actor puts one thing on from the closet – e.g. apron – to become* MUM, *and a female actor puts one thing on – e.g. tie or hat – to become* DAD. *They speak to the audience.*

MUM. Once upon a time there was a girl.

DAD. We'd read to her every night.

MUM. Once upon a time there was a little girl who lived in a house.

DAD. She'd cry all the time. Nights, days, you name it.

MUM. Isn't anything else to name. Nights and days. That's everything.

DAD. She cried all the time.

MUM. First day wouldn't stop crying, in the hospital. Nurse said, I remember, she said 'Think this is bad, wait till she's a teenager.'

DAD. Slamming doors.

MUM. You have hopes for your child.

DAD. Headphones attached to her ears.

MUM. Dreams for your child.

DAD. Don't even know what her ears look like any more.

MUM. Big plans for your child.

DAD. Weeks without saying a word to us.

MUM. And you plan for all that other stuff, the awkward years they want nothing to do with you, but this.

DAD. Silence.

MUM. This you don't plan for. This is not in the handbook.

DAD. Can't remember the last time you actually saw her.

MUM. It's not even in the secondary reading.

DAD. Maybe she was never there.

MUM. After the incident. When she was thirteen. We went on this course.

DAD. It was counselling.

MUM. To try to understand why she tried to… well…

Beat. This is uncomfortable for them.

DAD. We all went. The whole family. To Dr Learner.

MUM. She wasn't a doctor.

DAD. She had a PhD.

MUM. In anthropology.

DAD. Sociology.

MUM. She sent us on this course. They may as well have called it the Centre for Failed Parents, the sorry lot of us, doing role-plays.

DAD. As I recall you refused to take part.

MUM. I am forty years old – I think it's a bit ridiculous I should have to prance around finding my inner teen. This is the best part, they had these situations, and I had to play my daughter, while some out-of-work actor gets trolleyed in to play me. Show me how to communicate with my child. Girl's half my age, can't even get a walk-on part in *Hollyoaks* and she's telling me how to be a mother.

DAD. The point is

MUM. The point is *this* was not covered on the course. Not even mentioned. I should go ask for a refund.

DAD. It's not like we knew then anyway that's what this was all about, why she – he, he. I find the pronouns so confusing. Spend half the day practising, in my head, so I don't get it wrong.

MUM. Once upon a time there was a girl. She was breastfed and burped and rocked to sleep and everything the manual tells you to do. And she grew up and became a princess.

DAD *gives her a look.*

What?

Scene Four

Glastonbury Festival. DEAN *and* LAURA *by a tent. Shorts, hoodies and wellies.* AMY *returns with beers. She wears leather boots.*

AMY. Think I just saw sir.

LAURA. Is that one of the bands? Are they cute?

AMY. As in Sir sir. As in Mr Woolner.

LAURA. Eww, isn't that like, isn't there like an age limit? To ban teachers' entry? It's not on seeing teachers in the summer hols. Glastonbury should be off-limits.

DEAN. How'd you get beers?

LAURA. Last thing I want to see in my hols is Mr Woolner putting on factor forty-five in a vest top.

AMY. Sister's ID. I think he's kinda cute.

LAURA (*fixes hair, looking round*). Who?

AMY. Mr Woolner.

DEAN. Gross.

LAURA. Mega-gross. And you're not allowed to say stuff like that – you're engaged.

AMY. He was wearing a motorbike jacket.

LAURA. Ew, literally mid-life crisis. When I reach middle-age, I'm going to embrace it. Start wearing polo necks, and my hair in a bun, and big pants.

AMY. God I'd rather die.

LAURA. No you wouldn't.

AMY. I would. Literally.

LAURA. No. Not literally.

AMY. Literally. I'm gonna die young, forever remembered like this, never age, like all the greats – Buddy Holly, Kurt Cobain, James Dean. Forever young and beautiful.

LAURA. Yeah, but those are all guys. Can you think of one famous girl who went young?

AMY. Amy Winehouse.

LAURA. Yeah, but do you really, I mean honestly, Amy Winehouse? Do you really wanna go out like her?

AMY. Thanks, Laura, now I'm now destined to a long unhappy future growing old. At least I'll age gracefully. No big pants for me.

LAURA. No, sorry. Men age like red wine. Women age like milk.

AMY. Did you actually just – you can't say things like that any more, this isn't 1950.

LAURA. Speaking of which we've thought of the perfect theme for your wedding.

DEAN. We have?

AMY. There's a theme?

LAURA. As your maids of honour

AMY. Maid and male of honour

LAURA. We thought that

DEAN. We haven't actually discussed this actually.

AMY. I don't know that I want a theme.

LAURA. You *have* to have a theme. Literally everyone has one. Everyone.

AMY. Maybe we should check with Kyle. The wedding's all kind of his thing, you know.

LAURA. But you're the bride – when will he be here?

DEAN. Kyle's coming?

AMY. Didn't I say? They got last-minute tickets.

DEAN. They? Who's they?

Pause.

Fuck you, Amy.

AMY. I could've sworn I told you.

DEAN. Fuck you, Amy.

AMY. Can't we all be grown-ups. I mean I'm getting married for God's sake.

DEAN. Good for you. You grow up then.

AMY. Shit. I'm getting married. Bit scary when you say it out loud.

DEAN. You could've warned me, Amy.

AMY. Shit.

LAURA. You literally haven't talked to each other in months. You gonna spend the last year of college ignoring each other? Speaking for myself, just me, it's a bit awkward for the rest of us, don't you think, Amy?

AMY. I'm gonna be a wife.

LAURA. I'm happy to be the mediator. My mum's a psychologist y'know.

DEAN. I remember. She came in to give us all counselling in year ten when the science teacher ran off with that year eleven girl.

AMY. Whatever happened to her?

LAURA. She became a Scientologist. Had twins.

DEAN. How do you know this?

LAURA. My mum counselled the teacher.

AMY. I thought he's in prison.

LAURA. No, he's in Slough.

KYLE *and* JOSH *enter with bags of food.*

KYLE. If food be the music of love, eat on.

AMY. Thank God, I'm starving.

JOSH. We've got Tesco's finest breadsticks, falafel, and hummus.

LAURA. Didn't you bring any real food?

JOSH. Oh. Hi.

DEAN. Oh. Hi.

Awkward pause. AMY *has already dug into the hummus.*

AMY. Hummus anyone?

No?

LAURA. Did you bring any sausage rolls?

KYLE. Amy's a vegan.

AMY. Sweetie, I'm not *a* vegan. I'm vegan.

KYLE. Well yeah.

AMY. Well no. It's derogatory. You don't say *a* black, *a* gay.

KYLE. I do actually.

LAURA. Oh my God, the wedding's not going to be vegan is it?

AMY (*simultaneous*). Yes.

KYLE (*simultaneous*). No.

LAURA. It doesn't really fit with the theme though.

KYLE. What theme?

AMY. So, what, we're going to have dead animals on every table are we?

KYLE. My mum just wants roast chicken, you make it sound like we're gonna have some taxidermy centrepieces.

JOSH. That'd be pretty cool actually. (*Off* AMY*'s 'kill you' look.*) Or not.

LAURA. We were thinking it could be

DEAN. Again there's no we

LAURA. Like a *Grease* wedding.

JOSH. As in a fry-up?

LAURA. As in the musical.

KYLE. I hate musicals. There's just so much… singing.

LAURA. Well it could just be like a fifties theme.

AMY. You just want to wear that stupid poodle skirt you bought and can't wear.

LAURA. They were supposed to make a comeback.

DEAN. Fifties, I like it.

KYLE. We could get like a fifties band.

AMY. Or maybe you could just get some battery hens and force them to play the bongos with their broken beaks and I can wear a piglet-skin dress with leather shoes!

LAURA. You're actually wearing leather shoes. Literally. Like right now.

KYLE. You actually are though, babe.

AMY. I had them before, okay! God! I'm not marrying you! (*Stomps off.*)

KYLE. Wait. Was she being serious? Shit. Babes! (*Goes after her.*)

LAURA. I hope they're okay. The venue's non-refundable is all. And I've already cut the price tag off my skirt.

DEAN. People get married for less.

LAURA. I better go mediate. (*Exits.*)

JOSH *attempts to set up the tent. He quickly becomes exasperated with it and its lack of cooperation. Beats the tent with one of the poles.*

JOSH. Dumb-ass piece of… piece of… plastic, piece of carrier bag!

DEAN. Easy, cowboy, or someone's gonna call a hotline for victims of tent abuse.

JOSH. She was asking for it, your honour. She'd unzip the door to anyone.

Sorry, not funny.

DEAN. No.

It's inside out.

JOSH. How do you mean?

DEAN. The bit that's currently on the inside should be on the outside.

JOSH. Oh.

He begins to put it up. Still struggling. DEAN *wordlessly assists him, and together they quickly put it up.*

Thanks. I would have managed eventually y'know?

DEAN. No. You forget we've been camping before.

Beat.

JOSH. So you're talking to me?

DEAN. So you're talking to me?

JOSH. I never stopped talking to you.

DEAN. I never stopped talking to you.

JOSH. Then why weren't you talking to me?

DEAN. Cos you weren't talking to me.

JOSH. Only cos I thought you weren't talking to me.

DEAN. Why would you think that?

JOSH. Cos you sent a text and that was it.

DEAN. That was it cos you never wrote back.

JOSH. What was I meant to write?

Pause.

DEAN. You're staring. What?

JOSH. Spent the last few months avoiding eye contact that I've not properly got to really… you've got the same eyes.

DEAN. No shit, Josh.

JOSH. The rest of you, it's you, but not. But you still look… still look –

DEAN (*defensive*). *Look* what?

JOSH. Look fit. You still look fit. But as a boy. You're a fit boy.

Beat.

I'm not gay.

DEAN. I know.

JOSH. Just saying, cos don't want you to think

DEAN. I know, Josh. I know.

JOSH. I know you do.

I bloody hate festivals. Buncha smelly muddy pissheads in wellies pretending to have a good time.

DEAN. So why'd you come?

Beat. [*Because I knew you'd be here.*]

Your tent's a bit crap. Sure it's gonna keep you dry?

JOSH. Got nowhere else to sleep. Do I?

He looks to his tent.

Is that you? Inside out? Outside in?

DEAN. Maybe.

JOSH. I'm trying here, Izz – Dean. I'm trying. Cos I don't, you don't just wake up one morning and…!

DEAN. I did. I did just wake up one morning and.

JOSH. Well that's that then.

DEAN. I don't have to explain myself to you.

JOSH. No. But you should. You should want to. As your, as your former

DEAN. As the artist formerly known as boyfriend.

JOSH. Do you always have to make a joke of everything? If you were gonna change something, couldn't it at least have been your sarcasm?

Why are you smiling? It's not funny.

DEAN. It is. Us. Here. This. I dunno.

JOSH. Right. Well you have a little laugh. I'm gonna join the others.

He goes to leave, but stops when DEAN *starts speaking.*

DEAN. I woke up.

I woke up. I showered.

I woke up. I showered. And then the mirror was just there. Suddenly there. Only it had always been there, but I'd, somehow, I'd managed to never look. To never really look. Little tricks to avoid myself. But this day, I was there reflecting back, naked. And it took a minute, prolly only seconds, but felt like ages before I realised it was me. My body. And without even thinking I crossed my arms, have you ever noticed – how I always do that? For as long as I can remember I've always been doing that. And I tried to make them go away. I tried to look away. Because I'd never really looked. But I couldn't. This was me. And I hated it. Because it wasn't me. Do you understand? My little cousin Adam, you met him at my aunt's wedding, and she's always complaining because Adam won't leave it alone – he's five and he won't stop playing with his willy. Always investigating. I never did. Never investigated my own body. Why? Why is that? I'm standing in front of this mirror, the steam fading away, making the image clearer and clearer, this girl, this woman staring back at me. And it was like everything clicked into place. People say your life flashes before your eyes before you die, well I wasn't dying but suddenly everything in my life was playing back.

MUM *and* DAD *appear, speak to audience. They can't be seen by* DEAN *or* JOSH.

MUM. My mother gave her a doll for her sixth birthday, the one, what's the one, everyone had it, everyone had it but it was hard to get, but my mother had gone all over town just to get one, and she opened it up and started screaming: 'I don't want a doll! I don't want a doll!' Threw it at Granny. It landed in the lasagne. We laughed about it the next day. But. Well, the lasagne was ruined.

DAD. When she was five, I took her to the toilets, at a fair, into the men's, cos Mum wasn't there. At first she tried to use the urinal. A week later she asked: 'Daddy, when am I going to grow a willy?'

MUM *and* DAD *disappear again.*

DEAN. And in the mirror it all just suddenly made sense. Why I'd always felt a bit… wrong. And suddenly in my head, everything was… right. I'd never investigated, because I knew I wouldn't like what I found.

Music can be heard distantly. JOSH *suddenly does an impromptu dance move – cartwheel, flip, weird dance?*

What was that?

JOSH. Dunno. Couldn't think of what to say…

DEAN. I can't believe they're getting married. Christ. They should be locked up.

JOSH. Both their parents are letting them.

DEAN. They should be locked up too.

JOSH. I'm still in love with you.

Pause.

Then thunder. It starts to piss it down.

Shit.

Each goes into their respective tents.

Shit, there's a – I'm getting – there's a bloody hole.

DEAN. It's just water.

JOSH. This is a new shirt. It's a bloody bathtub in here.

DEAN. If you're gonna be a girl about it. Just come here.

He goes and sits in DEAN*'s tent. They're close together. Their legs touching.*

JOSH. You've got leg hair. Is that the um, the hormones?

DEAN. I've always had leg hair, douchebag. I just used to shave it.

JOSH. Right. Yeah.

They watch the rain.

JOSH *watches* DEAN.

DEAN. What?

JOSH. I bloody hate festivals.

DEAN. Yeah. Me too.

Scene Five

Some actors enter the stage. Put on suit jackets or ties or something smart. This is the school's SENIOR MANAGEMENT TEAM. *Divide the lines amongst actors as desired.*

SMT. We the school

We the SMT of the school

must tell you

want to tell you

that we one hundred percent support you

one hundred percent of the way.

We the SMT

need to stress

want to stress

that we are a very tolerant school

meaning we will show no tolerance

for those who are not tolerant

meaning we're tolerant of everyone

except those who aren't tolerant.

Meaning we the SMT

and you

we're all going to go through this together.

It's a first for all of us.

We're all transitioning together.

Well not literally.

Not literally, no, we won't actually

my wife wouldn't…

Not actually

not literally
but in a manner of speaking.

What we mean
the key
yes the key. This is a key
to the staff toilets
should you
if you feel
if you'd like to use those
if it would make you more comfortable.
It's up to you.
Absolutely. We're not saying
we're definitely not saying you can't use the student loos
definitely not
meaning where you pee is up to you
where you pee is your business
pee where you like.
Within reason.
Within reason.
Pee wherever suits you.
Not literally. You can't actually start peeing in the corridor.
What it boils down to
what it comes down to is…

Ofsted are coming.
Literally.

Actually.

Some time in the next school year.

And there'll be an assembly for them.

Not *for*, just while they're here.

For the students, we don't do things just for Ofsted.

About diversity, and inclusivity, and tolerance.

And we, the SMT, would like you, Dean, to make a speech.

What do you say?

School is accepting but obviously awkward and not completely understanding

Scene Six

Boys' toilets at school. DEAN *pees at a urinal.* JOSH *watches.* DEAN *finishes, and turns around.*

DEAN. How long have you been standing there?

JOSH. Why are you avoiding me?

DEAN. Were you watching me? That's a bit –

JOSH. Been trying to speak to you all week, you haven't answered my texts, I have to follow you into the boys' toilets to actually get you to talk to me.

DEAN. That's a bit

JOSH. Determined.

DEAN. I was gonna go with stalkerish.

JOSH. Ever since the festival

DEAN. There's never any soap in here.

JOSH. I thought it was good, I thought we were

DEAN. Why is there never any soap?

JOSH. And then in the morning you went all

DEAN. You don't have any hand sanitiser, do you?

JOSH. Do you have to be such a dick about it?

You just gonna pretend nothing happened? That we didn't – ?

DEAN. Yes that's exactly what I'm going to do.

JOSH. I don't get you, Dean.

DEAN. Sometimes I don't get me either, alright.

Can you move please? I have class.

JOSH. No. Not until we – you don't get to just, just make all the decisions. You don't get to pretend it didn't happen. I, I am part of that decision.

DEAN. Josh, move.

JOSH. No.

DEAN. You gonna trap me in here?

JOSH. Yes. Yes that's exactly what I'm going to do. (*Stands in a pose as barrier, reposes to something tougher – hands on hips? – reposes again, can't quite get right.*)

DEAN *laughs.*

Don't laugh. This is serious. This is, this is kidnapping, this is illegal, this is this is, this is fucking *no one's leaving this fucking toilet till I get some answers*!

Beat. He realises how ridiculous he is.

Christ, I can't even pull off a takeover in the school toilets. How am I ever going to be a detective?

Your fly.

DEAN*'s fly is undone.*

DEAN. Thanks, Miss Marple.

(*Re: crotch/peeing.*) It's a tube thing before you ask. That's how.

JOSH. I wasn't going to ask.

DEAN. Yes you were.

JOSH. No.

DEAN. You were thinking it.

JOSH. I was thinking it, but I wasn't going to ask.

Beat. They smile.

DEAN *takes an audition poster off the wall/stall door.*

DEAN. The year nines are doing *Twelfth Night* again.

Woolner has a limited repertoire.

JOSH. Worked for us, didn't it?

'Want me to help you practise your lines?'

DEAN. You're such a cheeseball.

JOSH. Rehearsed it the whole night before. Couldn't even look at you. 'Want me to help you practise your lines?'

DEAN. You're an idiot.

JOSH.

'…what a deal of scorn looks beautiful
In the contempt and anger of his lip!'

DEAN.

'We men may say more, swear more,
But indeed our shows are more than will; for still we
prove
Much in our vows, but little in our love.'

JOSH. I thought we were good.

DEAN. Your acting was a bit ropey.

JOSH. At the festival. I thought we were back on track. When we

DEAN. I'd been drinking.

JOSH. You invited me to sleep in your tent.

DEAN. Yours had turned into a wading pool.

JOSH. You said, after, you said how we'd still go away gap year. 'Course' you said. Go to Thailand like we planned.

Bum around on the beach, get shitfaced, bathe in the sea, go see the Lady Boys of Bangkok, / swim in the

DEAN. / I definitely never said anything about the Lady Boys of / Bangkok

JOSH. / and then we get back to school and you go all –

I won't just pretend it didn't happen. The festival.

DEAN. But you want to pretend it's the same as before. Like nothing's changed.

JOSH. That's not true.

DEAN. You're not gay, Josh. You said it yourself.

JOSH. So?

DEAN. So! What do you mean so?

JOSH. I mean so. Why do you have to put a label on everything? I want you. What does the rest of it matter?

DEAN. It just. It matters.

JOSH. What are you so afraid of?

DEAN. I don't know. I don't…

I hated *Twelfth Night* you know.

JOSH. What?

DEAN. I'm just saying.

Everyone all happy, getting married, just hated it. And that line. When Viola says: *Conceal me what I am*. I always thought it should be: *Conceal me what I'm not*. *Conceal me what I'm not*.

This is who I am, Josh. It can't be like before. I'm trying to protect you.

JOSH. From what?

DEAN. Me. Them. It'll be worse for you, Josh. Worse for you than me. They'll give you a harder time than me.

JOSH. Fuck 'em. Fuck 'em.

DEAN. And if it's not them, it'll be me. The hormones, they're, I'm moody, and tired, and my sex drive is out of control –

JOSH. I can cope with that.

DEAN. And I'm, emotionally, I'm on a fucking other planet, I'm a concrete wall, and when I'm not, I'm a goddamn waterfall, I just start, out of nowhere, and I've got like a hundred doctors, and my fucking parents, and my fucking sister, and the fucking school and their fucking equality policies they want *me* to update, and I'm a complete – like you said, I'm a complete dick. Okay? Right now, I'm just a, a complete fucking dick.

JOSH. Well be my fucking dick. Be my dick, Dean.

Beat. DEAN *takes* JOSH*'s hands. They're back together.*

Some stories have a happy ending, Dean. You're allowed to give yourself a happy ending.

Scene Seven

MUM *and* DAD.

DAD. I bought lots of books.

MUM. I read her lots of books.

DAD. I like to read up on things to really understand, what's what – I'm a scientist, how my brain works.

MUM. You're not a – you work in computers.

DAD. Need to understand the logic. The whys and wherefores. Only no one really knows.

MUM. There's no science.

DAD. There are theories that it's the shape of the brain. The bed nucleus of the stria terminalis. Or could just be her environment. How she was nurtured.

MUM. No, we did everything by the book.

DAD. I've read every book on the subject. And you know what I learned in the end?

MUM. Once upon a time, there was a girl. The girl was given everything she was supposed to. Pretty dresses, and pretty toys, and pretty ballet slippers. And pink wallpaper.

DAD. Left her alone for a day, seven hours, she was ten. Walked to B&Q and back. We came home. She'd painted over all the wallpaper. She'd painted her room black.

MUM. Ballet class and gymnastics and horseback riding – we signed her up for everything, so don't give me your nurture bullshit. She sucked at my nipples for eighteen months. What the hell did you do?

DAD. There was a point I thought she might be – it crosses your mind as a parent – I thought she might be a lesbian.

MUM. We both did.

DAD. She was never a girly girl.

MUM. They were playing classics at the Picturehouse. She was thirteen, just after she – around the time of the counselling.

DAD. Dr Learner.

MUM. And so we made an effort. A family trip. *Rebel Without a Cause*. And she fell in love. Poster on her wall of James Dean. And I thought, yes, yes! Normal. This is what normal teenage girls do – they put posters on their wall.

DAD. Arrived one day. In the post. An A1 James Dean.

MUM. We followed the books and we succeeded.

DAD. Two months earlier she'd tried to kill herself. I think she'd self-harmed before, but we didn't know.

Pause.

MUM. Once upon a time…

Once upon…

There's a line in the film. *Rebel Without a Cause*. The dad of the girl says: 'All of a sudden she's a problem.' And she, the wife, says: 'She'll outgrow it dear, it's just the age. It's just the age where nothing fits.'

I've only seen the film once. But I still remember that line.

Scene Eight

DEAN*'s room and various doctors' offices. We watch three actors put on doctor's coats to become* MONROE, BOGART *and* BRANDO. *The scene should become more and more physical and surreal as it goes on. It should feel by the end that* DEAN *is engaged in a workout.*

MONROE. Diagnosis is important, to get access to treatment

BOGART. Transgender, Gender Dysphoria

BRANDO. Gender Identity Disorder

MONROE. Gender non-conformity.

BOGART. Assessments:

MONROE. Psychodiagnostic and psychiatric

BOGART. Social

BRANDO. Physical.

MONROE. To prepare you for

BOGART. Full transition

MONROE. Treatment

BRANDO. Surgery.

BOGART. Take a seat

MONROE. Take a seat

BRANDO. Take a seat.

JAMES DEAN. Look how you're sitting. Lean back. Like you own the place. More.

But don't slouch.

Put an arm on the back of the chair.

Let your wrist flop. Not that much.

Open your legs. Guys take up a lot of room.

Yeah. Sorta. Look, watch me, kid.

Your turn.

DEAN *copies his sit.*

You look like you're constipated.

DEAN. It's easy for you, alright. It's natural. You don't need to think about it.

JAMES DEAN. You think this is natural? It's all performance, kid. I learned it. Now try again.

MONROE. When did you first have dysphoric feelings?

BOGART. Will your parents be coming to any appointments? It would be useful to speak to them as well.

MONROE. Are you in a relationship? Girlfriend? Boyfriend?

BRANDO. I'll refer you to Dr Monroe

MONROE. I'll refer you to Dr Bogart

BOGART. I'll refer you to Dr Brando

BRANDO. It'll be just fine, Dean. Just breathe.

JAMES DEAN. Breathe deep. Gotta speak from the back of your throat, your chest.

Hum down, head down, then bring your head up.

Again.

Again.

Really open your throat.

MONROE. Need you to open up. Need to ask how it felt? How it feels?

JAMES DEAN. 'Boy if I had one day when I didn't have to be all confused and I didn't have to feel ashamed of everything. I felt that I belonged someplace, you know?'

DEAN. That's my favourite part of the film.

JAMES DEAN. Your turn.

DEAN (*American accent*). Boy if I had one day

JAMES DEAN. Not in my accent, crazy.

DEAN (*back in own accent*). Boy if I had one day

JAMES DEAN. Lower.

DEAN. Boy if I had one day

JAMES DEAN. Lower

DEAN. Boy if I had

JAMES DEAN. Guys got less inflection. More monotone.

DEAN. Boy if I had one day when I didn't have to be all confused and I didn't have to feel ashamed of everything. I felt that I belonged someplace, you know?

MONROE. I do. Yeah.

JAMES DEAN. Yeah. We're getting there.

MONROE. Dean. Can I ask about the scars on your arms?

DEAN *standing*. BRANDO *measures his chest*.

JAMES DEAN. What you doin' with your arms?

DEAN. I dunno!

JAMES DEAN. Monotone.

DEAN. I dunno.

JAMES DEAN. Well gotta put 'em somewhere. Put your hands in your pocket. Walk.

Not so straight, your hips'll sway. Imagine an invisible line.

DOCTORS *roll out the measuring tape on the floor.*

You wanna be walking a foot either side of that.

DEAN *does*.

BRANDO. Keep the partying to a minimum. Drugs, alcohol – they can mess with your testosterone.

JAMES DEAN. T-time.

Hands needle. DEAN *injects*.

BRANDO. Some of it's irreversible. You can expect

DOCTORS. Body-hair growth

Scalpel hair loss

Increased muscle mass

Body-fat redistribution

Skin oiliness

Clitoral enlargement

JAMES DEAN. Lean back.

DOCTORS. Body-hair growth

JAMES DEAN. Hum down

DOCTORS. Scalpel hair loss

JAMES DEAN. Monotone

DOCTORS. Increased muscle mass

JAMES DEAN. Pocket

DOCTORS. Body-fat redistribution

JAMES DEAN. Invisible line

DOCTORS. Skin oiliness

JAMES DEAN. Lower

DOCTORS. Clitoral enlargement

JAMES DEAN. Again.

Lean back

DOCTORS. Body-hair growth

JAMES DEAN. Hum down

DOCTORS. Scalpel hair loss

JAMES DEAN. Monotone

DOCTORS. Increased muscle mass

JAMES DEAN. Pocket

DOCTORS. Body-fat redistribution

JAMES DEAN. Invisible line

DOCTORS. Skin oiliness

JAMES DEAN. Lower

DOCTORS. Clitoral enlargement

JAMES DEAN. Again.

BOGART. Have you seen Dr Monroe yet?

LAURA *and* JOSH *appear.*

JAMES DEAN (*keeps repeating underneath* LAURA, JOSH, *and* DOCTORS). Invisible, pocket, mono, lean, low, hum, T, again.

LAURA. Don't forget to bring a naughty parcel for the hen do. I've got her this hilarious penis-hat to wear all evening. It's gonna be a riot.

JOSH. Don't forget to bring booze for the stag. We've got him a naughty nurse's outfit he's got to wear all evening. And a fourteen-stone stripper. Gonna be brilliant.

BRANDO. For you it would be a bilateral mastectomy.

BOGART. Horizontal incisions across each breast.

MONROE. Peel skin

BRANDO. Remove mammary glands and fatty tissue

BOGART. Remove the areola, nipples

MONROE. Trim

BOGART. Then regraft them onto the chest in a male position

BRANDO. And you'll be home in time for supper.

MONROE. How does that sound?

JAMES DEAN *and* DOCTORS (*can be divided up or in unison*). Skin, trim, hair, T, lean, line, low, again.

Skin, trim, hair, T, lean, low, again.

BRANDO. I can schedule the chest surgery for 12th of June.

DEAN. Perfect. I've got a wedding late June.

BRANDO. Haha. No, not this June. 2016.

DEAN. Two years?

BRANDO. See you then.

Things speed up.

JAMES DEAN, DOCTORS, LAURA *and* JOSH (*can be divided up, or in unison*). Skin, trim, hair, T, lean, line, low, penis-hat, stripper, again.

Skin, trim, hair, T, lean, line, low, penis-hat, stripper, again.

Again. Again. Again. Again. Again.

DEAN *emerges, stands calmly, collected. At ease with his male self.*

DEAN. I felt that I belonged someplace, you know?

Beat.

JAMES DEAN, DOCTORS, LAURA *and* JOSH *all disappear and are replaced with* MUM, DAD *and* PRIVATE DOCTOR.

MUM. We agreed to go along

DAD. Dean had found a doctor, a private doctor.

MUM. She was very nice. I don't know what I was expecting. Frankenstein or something.

PRIVATE DOCTOR. Lots of people go private for the same reason. Shorter wait times.

DAD. She explained the procedure.

MUM. She *was* very nice.

PRIVATE DOCTOR. August 30th of this year, okay, Dean?

Don't forget, you'll need to pay by the 29th.

Five thousand nine hundred twenty-five pounds.

MUM. Once upon a time there was a witch who could turn the princess into anything.

DAD. Photos. What it would look like after. Without…

MUM. And I'm sorry. If that's what she wants to do. If she wants to mutilate her – then that's her prerogative. But we're certainly not going to bankroll it. When Sharon's daughter got a tattoo, do you think she paid for it?

DAD. This isn't a tattoo.

MUM. No. It's worse.

DAD. And these photos. All these *after* photos. And I thought

MUM. I'm sorry.

DAD. All these daughters. All these. Not just ours.

Scene Nine

DEAN*'s room.* DANI *is in there.* DEAN *has just entered.*

DEAN. Dani.

DANI. They're fighting again.

DEAN. What are you doing?

DANI. Nothing. Just y'know. Looking.

DEAN. Don't look through my stuff, alright?

DANI. I'm your younger sister. I'm meant to look through your stuff. I've done it for years.

DEAN. Well stop.

DANI. I thought maybe I could have your old clothes.

DEAN. I got rid of them already.

DANI. I noticed.

DEAN. Well… can you get out of here then?

Beat.

DANI *holds up a pair of boxers.*

DANI. Where did you get these?

DEAN. It's weird you going through my underwear.

DANI. *I'm* weird?

DEAN. Don't go through my stuff.

DANI. Where'd you get them?

DEAN. Why?

DANI. Topman. Says so on the price tag.

Why'd you steal them?

DEAN. What?

DANI. Cos they're expensive these. Especially when you only get six fifty an hour at Tesco. Expensive when you're saving up for an operation that costs six grand. Heard Dad say. Should buy your underwear from M&S. Much better value for money. Then you wouldn't have to steal.

DEAN. I don't know what you're talking about.

DANI *produces a security tag from her pocket.*

DANI. The security tag was on it.

DEAN. What do you want?

DANI. Why'd you steal them?

DEAN. I didn't.

DANI. You used to tell me stuff. But now you…

Fine. I'll just tell Mum and Dad and you can tell them why. (*Goes to leave.*)

DEAN. I panicked. I just… panicked. I was going to the till, and all these young men behind with their biceps, and rolled-up sleeves with bits of armpit hair sticking out, and designer beards, and the line of hair below their belly button when they absently start scratching, the band of their own Calvin Kleins and what if I get up there to pay and they…

DANI. And they know.

Beat. DANI *hands* DEAN *the underwear.*

I stole a dress last month cos it was ridiculously overpriced and I just wanted to see if I could. My friend taught me how to get the security tag off. (*Hands* DEAN *the security tag*.) So we're not that different, you and me.

(*Of poster.*) You sort of look like him.

DEAN. You think?

DANI. Sort of. Not really.

You remember when we all went to see that film all together? Don't think we've done anything all together since. Don't think we've been happy since.

I found this hidden in your wardrobe. (*Photo album*). The trip to the South of France when I was nine. Spent every day swimming. Look. We even had matching swimsuits. Do you remember? Cos if Mum bought it for you, she had to buy it for me. Do you remember? (*Laughs*.) And those hideous polka-dot long-sleeve dresses. So we cut the sleeves off – Mum was so angry. (*Laughs harder.*) Remember?

Look.

DEAN. I don't want to.

DANI. We were happy then.

DEAN. I wasn't. I wasn't happy then.

DANI. You were.

DEAN. No.

DANI. I was there. There are pictures! Look! We're smiling.

DEAN. Still

DANI. Not still. I was there!

DEAN. It wasn't the same for me.

DANI. You can't just change everything! You can't just change history, Izzy.

DEAN. Don't call me that.

DANI. They're my memories too. It's my life too. You can't just say it wasn't what it was and that's that – it's not some fucking video game you can just start again, new character, like none of it ever happened.

DEAN. I'm not saying it didn't happen. I'm just saying it wasn't the same for me.

DANI. That's not fair.

DEAN. No. But it's true.

DANI. We had matching swimsuits. We were a pair. The Cheeky Girls we called ourselves. (*Sings.*) 'We are the cheeky girls, we are the cheeky girls, you are the' –

DEAN. I hated that swimsuit.

DANI. We cut the sleeves off our dresses. Mum was so

DEAN. I wished I could've cut the whole thing up.

DANI. No. No, Izzy.

DEAN. Stop calling me that.

DANI. I have pictures, Izzy. We're smiling.

DEAN. Don't call me that.

DANI. Izzy, Izzy, Dizzy Izzy, Isabella!

DEAN *grabs the photo album. Rips a page from it. Scrunches/rips it up.*

Stop it! Stop it!

But DEAN *is on a mission.*

DANI *grabs the* JAMES DEAN *poster. Rips it down the middle. Runs out.*

DEAN *stops himself crying by focusing on mantra.*

DEAN. Invisible. Pocket. Mono. Lean. Low. Hum. T. Again. (*Calmly gets some scissors and cuts Izzy out of one of the photos as he repeats his mantra.*) Invisible. Pocket. Mono. Lean. Low. Hum. T. Again.

Scene Ten

Later. JOSH *has just entered. Cut-up photos are all over the floor.*

DEAN. What's five thousand nine hundred and twenty-five divided by two?

JOSH. Why does it look like Instagram vomited all over your room? I got you something.

DEAN. That's like… that's like three thousand a month, which is…

JOSH. A present.

DEAN. Fifteen hundred a week.

JOSH. Here.

DEAN. Which is like, with my six fifty a Tesco-hour, that's like, that's like

JOSH. Over two hundred hours.

DEAN. Two hundred hours. How the hell am I gonna work two hundred hours a week?

JOSH. You're not. There aren't two hundred hours in a week.

DEAN. What the hell am I meant to do?

JOSH. Are you not going to open my present?

DEAN. I could buy Lottery tickets.

JOSH. Dean.

DEAN. No you're right, that's completely, the odds are against me. Something less risky.

I could rob a bank.

JOSH. That's a brilliant idea.

DEAN. I could start an online business, and sell, sell – I could sell my old underwear. People pay big money for that you know.

JOSH. Dean, that's weird. Would you just open

DEAN. Yes, yes, I'll open the damn –

JOSH. There's a card.

DEAN (*opens it*). *Happy Anniversary*. Shit. Sorry. Shit.

JOSH. I don't care.

DEAN. I've just been completely wrapped up in

JOSH. I know. Honestly, I don't care.

DEAN (*opens gift*). *Lonely Planet Thailand*.

Sorry I didn't… Sorry. I'm crap.

JOSH (*affectionately*). I know. But you're my crap.

Look, they've got a whole chapter just on beaches. I thought we could start planning, y'know. Make it like a thing. A date. Each week we read one of the chapters, plan stuff.

DEAN. That sounds great. Though at this rate I won't be going.

JOSH. What do you mean?

DEAN. Well the tiny bit I've saved so far now's gotta go to the surgery, right? And if I can't get the money together by August, might have to have the surgery in the autumn or the winter.

JOSH. But we're leaving September 1st. That was the plan.

DEAN. Plan might have to change.

JOSH. You can have the surgery when you get back.

DEAN. That's not an option.

JOSH. I don't get what the hurry is.

DEAN. The hurry is I've already spent more than seventeen years like this.

JOSH. So what's one more year?

DEAN.…what?

JOSH. Maybe there's a reason the other wait list is two years, maybe you should just wait, you're meant to wait, and when we come back then you can see if you still…

DEAN. Still what?

JOSH.…there's nothing wrong with the way you are now.

DEAN. Oh my God. What you think – have you been hoping all this time I'd suddenly – what – that this is a phase or something?

JOSH. No.

DEAN. Oh I've seen sense, pass me the dress and make-up!

JOSH. No! That's not fair, Dean!

DEAN. What's not fair is having to wake up with these every day.

JOSH. I'm just saying how it is now is fine, you don't need to

DEAN. Fine for who?

JOSH. I'm trying here, Dean.

DEAN. Try harder.

JOSH. I have, I have, I have… well I've done loads haven't I? I'm here aren't I?

This affects both of us.

DEAN. This?

JOSH. And I'm sorry okay, but the thought of you, I'm okay with this, I love this, but the thought of you… mutilating your body… the thought of you without… it just, it just… freaks me out a bit.

Pause.

Dean.

DEAN. Get out.

JOSH. Don't be

DEAN. Get out, Josh.

JOSH. Let's talk about this. We'll figure something out.

DEAN. Stay away from me.

JOSH. I love you, Dean.

DEAN (*grabs scissors, holds out*). I said stay the fuck away from me.

Get out. (*Holds scissors to breasts.*) Or I'll cut them off myself.

JOSH *exits.*

DEAN *drops the scissors, starts crying. Sorts himself out in the mirror, repeating the mantra quietly to himself. Puts on some music. Buddy Holly's 'Everyday' like at the start. Gels his hair. Sprays some Lynx. Grabs a box/piggy bank. Takes a handful of cash from it.*

Scene Eleven

Voicemail.

SMT. Dean, we're just checking in
checking up really
making sure you're alright
making sure everything's alright
cos you've been absent for the past three weeks
so we wanted to make sure everything's okay…

And to inform you that the warning came
the call came
they're coming. Ofsted.
Which means the assembly
and you haven't given us your speech
which is fine
we totally trust you
absolutely
we just want to double-check you're still game
still on board
still alive and well.

And getting better.

Get well soon.

And if you could get better by Monday at 2 p.m. well then all the better.

Scene Twelve

DEAN*'s bedroom.* DEAN *looks a bit worse for wear. He's been partying hard the last couple of weeks.* LAURA*'s just entered.*

LAURA. What happened to your sick poster? I wanted to borrow it.

DEAN. What for?

LAURA. For the wedding. Would work brill-iant-ly with the decor. We could tape it.

DEAN. Um. Maybe.

LAURA. Who have you been out partying with?

DEAN. No one. I haven't.

LAURA. Sorry to just like, but I've left you like, literally a hundred messages. And no one's seen you. And you've missed a bunch of Tesco shifts.

DEAN. I've been here studying.

LAURA. Then why are you like dressed? Who have you been out with?

DEAN. I've been here.

LAURA. Dean.

DEAN. No one, Laura.

LAURA. Well you look a bit like a Pete Doherty Amy Winehouse love child.

So. Anyway. It's a bit awkward, but it's just best to come right out and say it. I'm a bit concerned about you and Josh.

DEAN. Oh. Thanks. But you don't need to be.

LAURA. But I do. Literally. Cos you're meant to be partners, walking back up the aisle after. And I'm concerned really, that your not talking could affect the dynamic.

DEAN. I'm not gonna get back together just for the sake of a wedding march.

LAURA. No. Course. That would be. Just. It might ruin the wedding. And I wouldn't want you to feel guilty, to feel responsible for ruining the most important day of their lives, that's all.

DEAN. I won't.

LAURA. Good, no. I just don't – like if it ends in divorce, don't want you to feel that you could've prevented it.

DEAN. Laura, I'm sure I can walk down the aisle with Josh, smiles and all.

LAURA. Good. Well that is a re-lief.

DEAN. Is that why you came over?

LAURA. No. I came. To show you… this! (*Pulls out poodle skirt and bow.*) What do you think?

DEAN. Yeah. You'll look great in it.

LAURA. Aww. Actually. It's not for me.

DEAN. Who's it for?

LAURA. Um. Well.

Pause.

Look, Dean. We all support you one hundred percent. Really. But this is their wedding day and I was chatting with Amy's mum and we both agree that, well, it could take the attention away from Amy and Kyle. Steal the limelight. You understand.

DEAN. I'm not wearing a skirt.

LAURA. It's just for one day.

DEAN. Do you know what you're asking me?

LAURA. Definitely. I definitely do. And I wouldn't if it were any other day.

DEAN. Does Amy know about this?

LAURA. She's got enough to worry about.

DEAN. I can't. No.

LAURA. Sure. I understand. It's just. Her mum said. Dean, you can't come to the wedding then. I'm really sorry.

I'll just. (*Leaves outfit.*) It's just one day, right? (*Exits.*)

DEAN *takes more money from his piggy bank/box.*

JAMES DEAN *appears.*

JAMES DEAN. I thought you were saving that money.

DEAN. I thought you were dead.

JAMES DEAN. Why? Cos she ripped the poster? I'm James Dean, buddy. I don't die. Not really.

Where are you going?

DEAN. I'm not.

JAMES DEAN. Who are you going with?

DEAN. What are you – my mum? If I'd wanted a mother figure I'd have dreamt up Audrey Hepburn or someone instead of you.

JAMES DEAN (*impersonating Hepburn*). 'I don't want to own anything until I find a place where me and things go together. I'm not sure where that is but I know what it is like. It's like Tiffany's.'

DEAN. You weren't even alive any more when that came out.

JAMES DEAN. Ouch. So why are you ignoring them? Your friends?

DEAN. I'm not ig– it's complicated. You wouldn't understand.

JAMES DEAN. Try me.

DEAN....

I just went in. I don't know what I was planning.

Sound/light from the bar/memory filters through, so it's like DEAN*'s there.*

To get shit-faced and forget him and snog some random maybe. But I... walked in, started talking to these young guys and they went to buy me a drink. And so I stood alone waiting in some crappy disco lights in a place that smelled of sweat and piss and farts, and I realised: they don't know anything about me. No one here does.

The disco light/sound goes, so we're back in the bedroom.

When I'm with them I feel like… I can forget.

JAMES DEAN. So you're just gonna cut off your friends? Forget them?

DEAN. But that's just it. Maybe they're not my friends. Maybe they're her friends.

Scene Thirteen

Men's toilets at a bar. DEAN *turns around from a urinal to find* KYLE *standing there.*

KYLE (*speaking into mobile phone as if it's a walkie-talkie*). Got him. Read: Subject has been located.

DEAN. Kyle, what are you doing here?

AMY *enters.*

KYLE (*speaking into mobile*). Subject identified.

AMY. You don't need to talk into your phone, I'm right here.

DEAN. Amy? You know you're in the men's toilets.

AMY. You know you haven't returned my calls or texts. Literally not a single one.

DEAN. Sorry, I've been… busy.

AMY. Is it drugs? Alcohol?

DEAN. What?

AMY. Well there must be some teenage cliché going on, which has forced us to stage an intervention.

DEAN. Oh. Is that what this is? How'd you find me?

AMY. Let's just say we have our ways, we know people.

KYLE. Your dad told us. Maybe we should go outside.

AMY. I'm not letting him out of my sight.

KYLE. But we're not really supposed to be in here. It's a bar.

AMY. What kind of bar has board games by the way? People getting pissed playing Connect Four.

KYLE. Just, if we get caught… I mean we're (*Whispers.*) under-age.

AMY. We're GETTING MARRIED for God's sake.

KYLE. And if you're caught in the gents', you could get arrested.

AMY. Well at least if I'm in prison I can stop talking about bloody table decorations. (*To* DEAN.) What's going on, Dean? You and Josh break up and then you stop talking to all of us, just disappear for like weeks and now Laura tells me you might not come to the wedding? We miss you, Dean.

DEAN.… I miss you guys too.

KYLE. Great. Sorted. Can we go? We're meant to be at an hors d'oeuvres tasting in like five minutes. (*To* DEAN.) We've been here like an hour. Amy didn't want to cause a scene in front of your new friends. So I've been waiting in here ages. One guy even called the manager to say there was a perv just sitting eating crisps in the toilets.

AMY. So who are they? That guy in the coveralls –

DEAN. Bart.

AMY. – is he your boyfriend?

DEAN. I guess he's…

JOSH *jumps out of one of the stalls* (*or wherever he's hidden*).

JOSH. That hipster-douche is your boyfriend?

DEAN. What the hell?

AMY. How long have you been hiding in there?

Kyle?

KYLE. I wanted someone to keep me company. (*To* JOSH.) You promised not to come out, mate.

AMY. I cannot believe you. I actually cannot like literally look at you right now, Kyle.

KYLE. You are looking at me.

AMY. It's a mirror. It doesn't count.

JOSH. Bart? Bart? As in Simpson?

DEAN. As in the Apostle actually. Bartholomew.

JOSH. You dumped me for a guy in a farmer's dungarees!

DEAN. Just because I find someone who's funny and chilled out and nice to me and doesn't hide in toilets –

JOSH. Does he know?

DEAN. Does he know what?

JOSH. Think if I go and tell him he'll still be so nice and funny and chilled out?

DEAN. Do you always have to be such a douche? All of the time?

JOSH. *I'm* a douche? I was peering at that guy for like the last hour. *He's* the douche. The king of douchebags. The *apostle* of douchebags.

KYLE. We should probably go, Amy.

AMY. I said I'm not looking at you.

KYLE. Yeah, but you can still hear me right?

AMY. If I hear the words seat cover or party favours once more, I swear to God I will divorce you before the wedding. Dean, can I ring you tonight? Will you pick up?

DEAN. Yeah. Yeah.

KYLE. Later, guys.

AMY *and* KYLE *exit*.

JOSH. We should talk.

DEAN. Ever noticed how your talks always need to happen in toilets? A metaphor for how piss-poor your talking is and the crap that comes out of your mouth. You're one of those turds that just won't go down. No matter how many times I flush you away you magically keep reappearing.

JOSH. I still care about you, Dean.

DEAN. Well stop. Hiding? Spying on me? What is wrong with you?

JOSH. What is wrong with *you*? You don't even know this guy.

DEAN. It has nothing to do with you, Josh.

JOSH. He could be a… proper mental case, kill you in the night.

DEAN. Well he hasn't killed me in the night yet.

JOSH. You've spent the night with him?

DEAN. What do you want, Josh?

JOSH. He could be part of some crazy paedophile ring.

DEAN. He's fifteen!

JOSH. What kind of name is Bartholomew anyway? What is he, a pirate?

DEAN. Yeah he's a pirate.

JOSH. Really?

DEAN. No, Josh. Now please just go home and leave us alone.

JOSH. Us? So you're an us?

DEAN. You know what, I don't care, stay here. Stay in the toilets. Write poetry about your genitals on the wall. (*Goes to leave.*)

JOSH. The plane tickets came.

DEAN. What?

JOSH. Thailand. Ordered them months ago. Well they arrived.

DEAN. No, no, you don't get to – this is what you do. I sort things out, I finally get shit in my life together and then you come along and fuck everything up again.

JOSH. I haven't – I'm just telling you the tickets arrived. And I don't know what to do. Tell me what to do, Dean.

DEAN. Sometimes you need to figure out what to do for yourself.

JOSH. Yeah. Yeah. I know. So I researched, I went online, and they say… it's normal.

Beat.

That I'm normal…

DEAN. You're…?

JOSH. How I reacted. And they… I think you need to be more patient with me.

I was, I was, all things considered, quite patient with you. And you were quite… selfish. So.

Pause.

And I think I've been, all things considered, I was, I've been a really tolerant person. So… yeah.

Pause. DEAN *moves slowly toward* JOSH, *stands close. Looks him in the eye.* JOSH (*and we*) *think* DEAN *might even hug him, or kiss him.*

But then DEAN *punches* JOSH *in the chest.*

Ow.

DEAN *hits* JOSH *again.*

Dean, that really hurts.

DEAN *hits him again.*

DEAN. Hit me.

JOSH. What?

DEAN. You wanna sort this out? Is that why you came here?

JOSH. I guess I –

DEAN. Is it?

JOSH. I s'pose.

DEAN. Then let's sort this out. Hit me.

JOSH. I'm not gonna –

DEAN *hits* JOSH *again.*

DEAN. What? Not gonna fight back? Be a man, Josh.

Hits him again.

JOSH. Ow, I'm not gonna

DEAN *hits him again.*

DEAN. You wanna sort this out? Keep your *tolerance* and fight back.

Hits again.

Fight.

And again.

Back.

JOSH. Stop! I'm not gonna hit a…

DEAN. A what? A what, Josh?

Hits again.

Say it! Say it!

Hits again.

JOSH. Stop it!

DEAN. I dare you. Say it!

Hits again.

JOSH. Stop it!

DEAN. Or

Hits.

hit me!

Keeps hitting.

'I'm not gonna hit a' – say it!

JOSH. Stop it!

JOSH *punches* DEAN *in the face*. JOSH *is as shocked as* DEAN *is*.

Shit. Sorry, sorry.

Pause.

DEAN (*genuine*). Thank you.

JOSH *goes*.

Scene Fourteen

School assembly. DEAN *has a black eye*.

DEAN. Good afternoon, students, teachers, and visitors from Ofsted.

Our school prides itself on tolerance. You can be who you want to be and we will tolerate you. It says so in a policy document in a drawer somewhere.

We learn in history about a black woman who decided one day to sit where she wanted to on a bus.

We learn about another woman who chained herself to Parliament.

We learn about some angry drag queens in a bar who fought back one night.

We learn that to be tolerant of every person is what we should aspire to. A badge of honour we can wear. *I am a tolerant person*.

Fuck tolerance.

Those people – the black lady on the bus, the woman in chains, those men in heels. They weren't fighting for tolerance. To be tolerated.

Because tolerance is horseshit.

Tolerance is the emptiest word in the dictionary.

Tolerate is what you do when someone's playing their music loudly on the bus.

Tolerate is what you do when someone's texting next to you in the cinema.

I don't want to be tolerated.

I want to be admired.

I want to be envied.

I want to be… loved.

Love me.

And if that's too much to ask. Then hate me.

But don't tolerate me.

Because tolerance means sweet fuck-all.

Dean wants to be more than tolerated

Scene Fifteen

AMY*'s bedroom.* KYLE *wears a wedding dress.*

JOSH. What the fuck?

KYLE. The band cancelled. Lead singer's getting a hip replacement.

JOSH. You're wearing a dress.

KYLE. Yeah.

JOSH. Okay.

KYLE. Yeah. So we've had to get a new band.

JOSH. Guess that's what happens when you get a band who were actually playing in the 1950s.

KYLE. So we've had to get impersonators. Buddy Hollister and the Abercrombies. Who were only born in like 1992… so just not as authentic – like what will these kids actually know?

JOSH. Why are you wearing a wedding dress?

KYLE. I don't like surprises. Couldn't leave it to chance.

JOSH. Oh. But why'd you put it on?

KYLE. Not sure.

JOSH. I thought it's bad luck to see the dress before.

KYLE. No, bad luck to see the bride *in* the dress.

JOSH. Groom in the dress is alright then.

KYLE *puts on the veil.*

Amy could walk in any second.

KYLE. No, she's watching *Don't Tell the Bride*, analysing all the things that could go wrong.

JOSH. Gonna be perfect.

KYLE. No surprise punches.

JOSH. There won't be.

KYLE. I mean you and Dean. Walking down the aisle.

Lift up the veil for me.

He does.

Is it easy?

JOSH. What?

KYLE. The lifting. What if it gets stuck?

JOSH. It won't.

KYLE. Gets caught in my cufflink and I can't raise it up?

JOSH. It's gonna be perfect. (*Starts to cry.*)

KYLE. Save it for the day, mate. Tears look great on camera.

JOSH. I fucked up. I royally – I always thought we'd get married. One day. Maybe after Thailand, uni. Find a flat, move in together. Grow old together. That was the plan. And I fucked it up.

KYLE. If you have a plan, you could make it happen.

JOSH. Sorry to break it to you, Kyle, but sometimes plans don't go to plan. Sometimes no matter what you wish for or plan for, what you get… you just get a shit fifties knock-off band.

There are days when I'm like I can do this. It's all normal. It's just a pronoun. And then suddenly I think it's all – and I think about Izzy and what we – and I don't know if I can handle it.

DEAN *appears on the other side of the mirror.*

KYLE. Do you love him?

JOSH.… Yeah. Yeah.

KYLE. Then unfuck it up.

Beat as DEAN *and* JOSH *stare at each other through the mirror. Then* JOSH *and* KYLE *go.*

Scene Sixteen

DEAN*'s bedroom.*

DEAN *holds up the poodle skirt and bow in front of him in the mirror.* JAMES DEAN *appears.*

JAMES DEAN. You know that skirt is so last century, right?

DEAN (*in an American accent*). 'Y'know. I bet you're a real yoyo.'

JAMES DEAN. 'I love you too.'

I saw your little speech.

DEAN. What'd you think?

JAMES DEAN. You've got balls. I'm proud of you, kid.

DEAN. It just sorta came out… the words.

BOTH. But it felt… I felt… for the first time I was really… me.

JAMES DEAN. Gimme those.

DEAN. I haven't got anything else to wear to the wedding.

JAMES DEAN (*takes off his jacket*). Here.

DEAN. What will you wear?

JAMES DEAN (*takes skirt and bow*). These.

JAMES DEAN *puts on the skirt, puts the bow in his hair.* DEAN *puts on the jacket.*

DEAN. Are you coming?

JAMES DEAN. Think I'll pass.

DEAN. Will you be here when I get back?

Pause.

JAMES DEAN. You'll be alright, kid. I think you'll be just fine.

Goodbye, Dean.

DEAN. Goodbye, Izzy.

DEAN *finds a dollar bill in the jacket pocket. Turns to give it to* JAMES DEAN *but he's gone. He puts the bill in his now empty piggy bank/box. A new start.*

Scene Seventeen

MUM *and* DAD.

DAD. Dani's not coping very well. So. She'll go live with her mother. She found a place not far. She didn't want the house.

MUM. She cut up all the photos. One night when everyone was sleeping. Cut herself out of all of them. If she was in the middle, if it was like a group photo, a family photo, she just cut out her head. Frame after frame after frame of… space. The space where my child used to be.

DAD. Book after book after book. And you know what I learned in the end?

MUM. But she missed one. (*Holds photo.*) Forgot to check my wallet. My baby. My baby girl.

DAD. I learned nothing. Cos no one has an explanation. But who needs an explanation? He's my… my…

MUM. My…

They switch clothes. So the female actor now plays MUM*, the male actor* DAD.

DAD. My… I still struggle saying *son*. When she was pregnant, I hoped it was a boy. I know you're not supposed to say that. But I did.

MUM. Once upon a time there was a girl. And then there wasn't.

DAD. He's my child. And I love him.

MUM. The guidebooks don't –

When a child dies you mourn. They say losing a child is the hardest of all deaths. They describe the feeling as – the noun they use is loss. Mourning. And when a child goes missing and is never found, you feel you're never able to rest, to properly just live. The noun they use is restlessness.

(*Starts to cry softly.*) My daughter is not dead. My daughter is not missing. But she is gone. And so I don't have the language to describe what I'm feeling. It's not in any of the books. There's no noun for that.

DAD. We went out for dinner the other day, the two of us, and the waiter comes over and he says: 'What can I get you lads to drink?' Two lads. Out for a drink.

MUM. There's a line in the film when she says: 'She'll outgrow it dear. It's just the age when nothing fits.'

I think that's a lie. Cos sometimes you turn forty-one, and still nothing fits like it's supposed to.

I hope… I hope he does. I hope Dean… fits.

* some closing about the parents. Parents understand more, even though it sounds like parents have divorced + sister is having a rough time

Scene Eighteen

Wedding reception. Everyone wears fifties outfits. DEAN *looks like* JAMES DEAN.

JOSH. Nice jacket.

DEAN. You think?

JOSH. I think.

DEAN. Amy's mum was giving me evils.

JOSH. No, it suits you. And the colour distracts from your eye.

DEAN. Is that meant to be funny?

JOSH. Yeah. No. I'm not sure.

DEAN. You're useless.

JOSH. I know. I'm sorry. 'Bout the eye.

DEAN. I asked for it. Literally.

JOSH. I'm still sorry. If it's any consolation, my chest still hurts like a bitch. That's some fist.

I liked your speech by the way.

DEAN. Laura wrote most of it. A speech to the tune of 'Summer Lovin' certainly wasn't my idea.

JOSH. I meant your speech at school.

DEAN. Oh. Got me two weeks' suspension.

JOSH. Still. It was kick-ass.

DEAN. Yeah.

JOSH. Bartholomew here? Or is he on a ship with a parrot looking for gold?

DEAN. I wouldn't know. Call me jean-ophobic but I just couldn't see a future with someone who wears dungarees.

JOSH. Here. (*Hands gift bag.*)

DEAN. Meant to get a gift for the bride and groom.

JOSH. Just open it.

DEAN *does. It's a McDonald's Happy Meal box.*

DEAN. Uhh… thanks… not sure weddings are really 'bring your own meal'.

JOSH. No, inside.

DEAN *opens the Happy Meal box. There's lots of money inside.*

DEAN.…

JOSH. Ever since that date we had at McDonald's, a couple years ago, when we first talked about spending our gap year together, I kept the box, to remind me. And whenever I could, I'd put savings in there, for our trip. Took it out in cash, put it under my bed, make sure I didn't spend it. There's about three and a half grand. It's over two grand short, but it's all I have.

DEAN. Josh.

JOSH. And before you even say it, you have to. Okay? You have to take it. August 30th.

DEAN. But Thailand.

JOSH. Thailand can wait.

Music lingers through from the dance floor. 'Teenager in Love' by Dion & The Belmonts.

DEAN. Josh, I don't know what to…

JOSH. One last dance?

DEAN. You're so melodramatic.

JOSH. Just shutup and dance with me.

DEAN *approaches. They're unsure where to put their hands… who's the boy in the dance? They try a couple things out and dance.*

I always thought Olivia should've married Viola, and Sebastian should've married Orsino… don't you think?

They keep dancing.

The song comes to an end, and changes to some cheesy wedding music.

I fucking hate weddings.

DEAN. Me too.

They stand close. Are about to kiss. When AMY *runs on in her wedding dress.*

AMY. Save me. If I have to smile for one more photo, I swear to God I'm gonna be the first bride to go berserk and murder all her guests on her wedding day. Kyle's made a spreadsheet of every photo that needs to be taken today. And who thought it would be a good idea to have a five-kilo wedding dress?

DEAN. At least you look beautiful.

AMY. I look like a Tinkerbell on steroids.

JOSH. Well at least you look better in it than Kyle.

AMY. What?

Are you eating McDonalds at my wedding?

KYLE *enters, with a clipboard.* LAURA *follows.*

KYLE. There you are. We're like eleven minutes behind. We're meant to have already cut the tofu cheesecake.

LAURA. And everyone's waiting for you to throw the bouquet.

AMY. I can barely lift my arms in this.

KYLE. Oh come on, my little soy chocolate button. I'll help you.

KYLE *leads her off,* AMY *mouths 'help' behind her.*

JOSH. I like your skirt, Laura.

LAURA. Thanks. You look good too. You both do. Really.

Don't want to miss the bouquet! (*Exits.*)

JOSH. Coming? It'll be fun.

DEAN. I'd rather spend eternity eating tofu cheesecake.

JOSH. Fair enough.

JOSH *exits. Pause.* DEAN *alone. Distant wedding sounds.*

DEAN. Once upon a time.

JOSH *runs back in.*

Josh.

Josh?

JOSH *grabs* DEAN. *Kisses him passionately.*

He runs back off. Before he's quite off:

Josh?

JOSH. Yes, Dean?

DEAN....

Catch that bouquet and I'll kill you.

JOSH *smiles. And exits.*

Once upon a time there was a boy.

End.

Other Plays for Young People to Perform from Nick Hern Books

Original Plays

100
Christopher Heimann,
Neil Monaghan, Diene Petterle

13
Mike Bartlett

BLOOD AND ICE
Liz Lochhead

BOYS
Ella Hickson

BRONTË
Polly Teale

BUNNY
Jack Thorne

CHRISTMAS IS MILES AWAY
Chloë Moss

COCKROACH
Sam Holcroft

DISCO PIGS
Enda Walsh

EARTHQUAKES IN LONDON
Mike Bartlett

EIGHT
Ella Hickson

GIRLS LIKE THAT
Evan Placey

HOW TO CURSE
Ian McHugh

HOW TO DISAPPEAR COMPLETELY AND NEVER BE FOUND
Fin Kennedy

I CAUGHT CRABS IN WALBERSWICK
Joel Horwood

KINDERTRANSPORT
Diane Samuels

MOGADISHU
Vivienne Franzmann

MOTH
Declan Greene

THE MYSTAE
Nick Whitby

OVERSPILL
Ali Taylor

THERE IS A WAR
Tom Basden

THE URBAN GIRLS' GUIDE TO CAMPING AND OTHER PLAYS
Fin Kennedy

Adaptations

ANIMAL FARM
Ian Wooldridge
Adapted from George Orwell

ARABIAN NIGHTS
Dominic Cooke

BAD GIRLS
Vicky Ireland
Adapted from Jacqueline Wilson

BEAUTY AND THE BEAST
Laurence Boswell

CORAM BOY
Helen Edmundson
Adapted from Jamila Gavin

DAVID COPPERFIELD
Alastair Cording
Adapted from Charles Dickens

GREAT EXPECTATIONS
Nick Ormerod and Declan Donnellan
Adapted from Charles Dickens

HIS DARK MATERIALS
Nicholas Wright
Adapted from Philip Pullman

THE JUNGLE BOOK
Stuart Paterson
Adapted from Rudyard Kipling

KENSUKE'S KINGDOM
Stuart Paterson
Adapted from Michael Morpurgo

KES
Lawrence Till
Adapted from Barry Hines

NOUGHTS & CROSSES
Dominic Cooke
Adapted from Malorie Blackman

THE RAILWAY CHILDREN
Mike Kenny
Adapted from E. Nesbit

SWALLOWS AND AMAZONS
Helen Edmundson and Neil Hannon
Adapted from Arthur Ransome

TO SIR, WITH LOVE
Ayub Khan-Din
Adapted from E.R Braithwaite

TREASURE ISLAND
Stuart Paterson
Adapted from Robert Louis Stevenson

WENDY & PETER PAN
Ella Hickson
Adapted from J.M. Barrie

THE WOLVES OF WILLOUGHBY CHASE
Russ Tunney
Adapted from Joan Aiken